AND SO THE ADVENTURE BEGINS

For:

____

Love:

____

Printed in the United States of America
First Printing, 2018

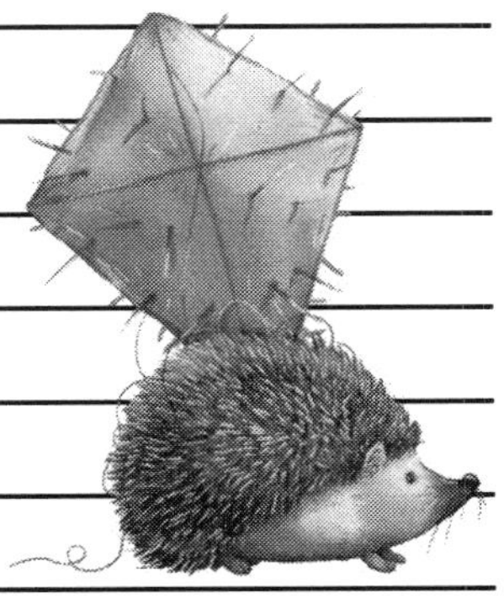

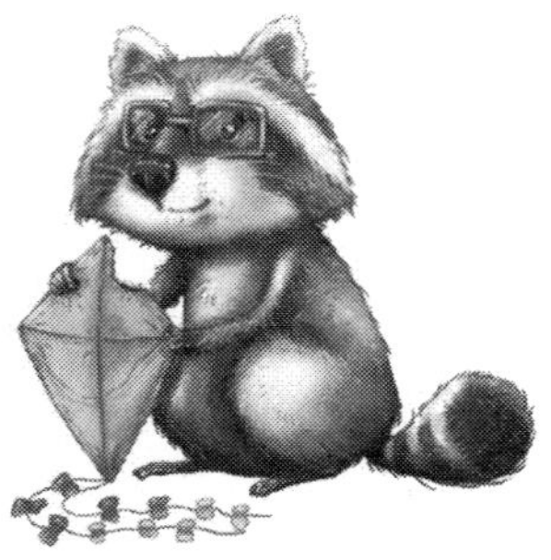

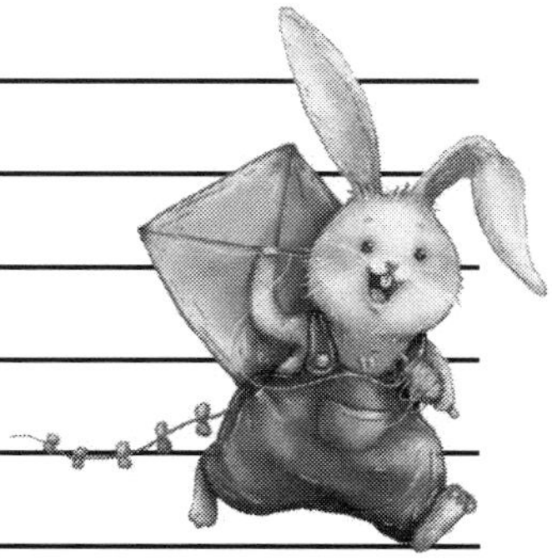

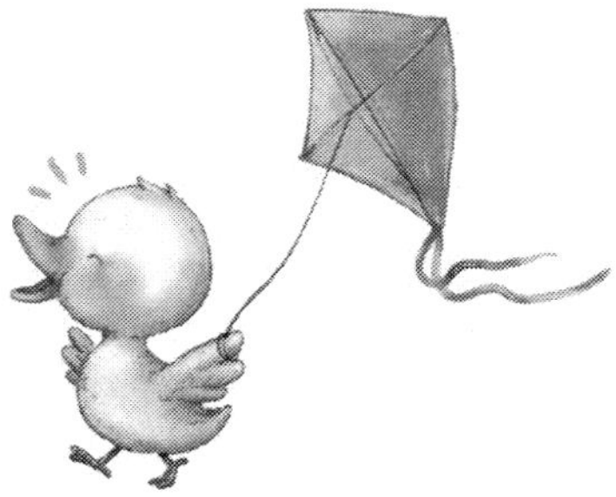

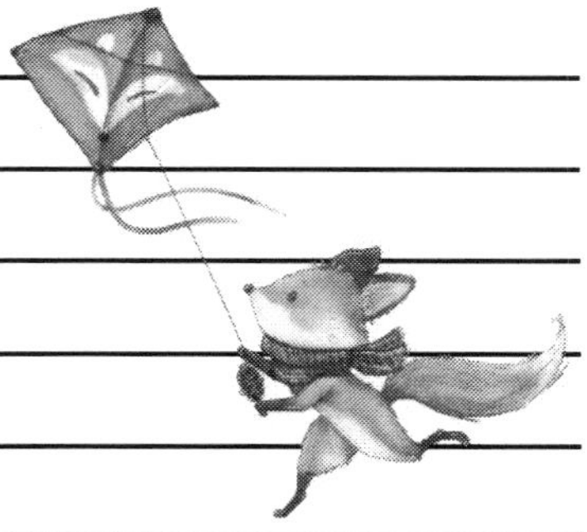

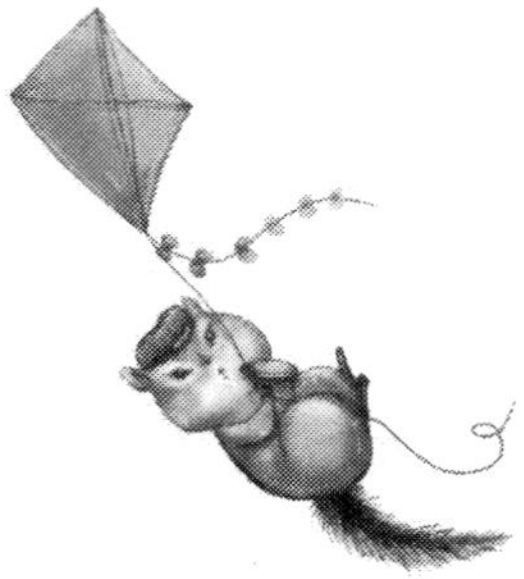

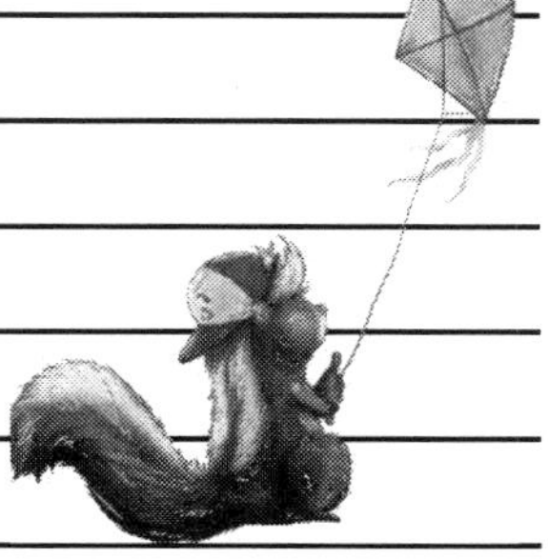

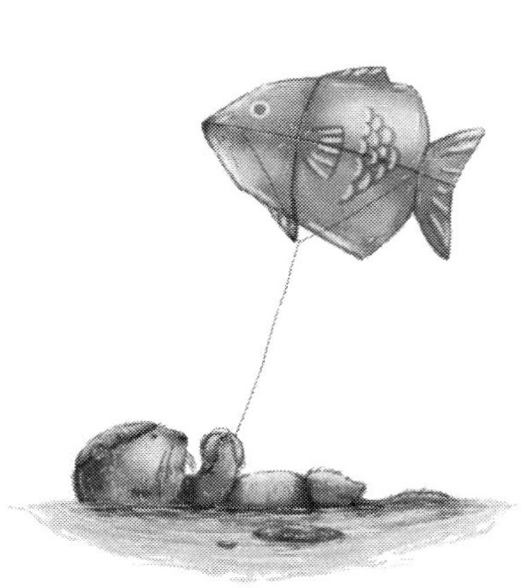

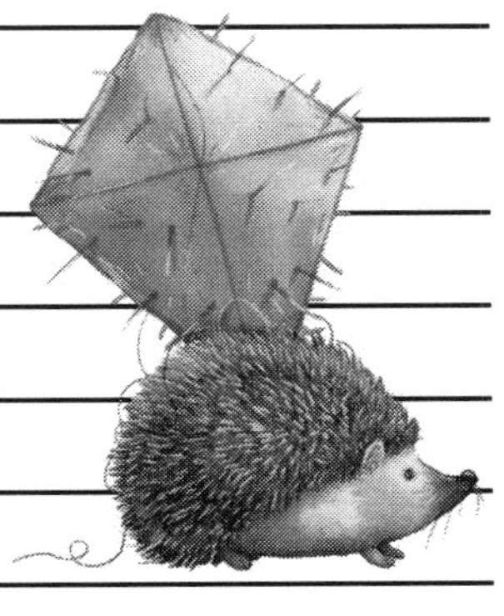

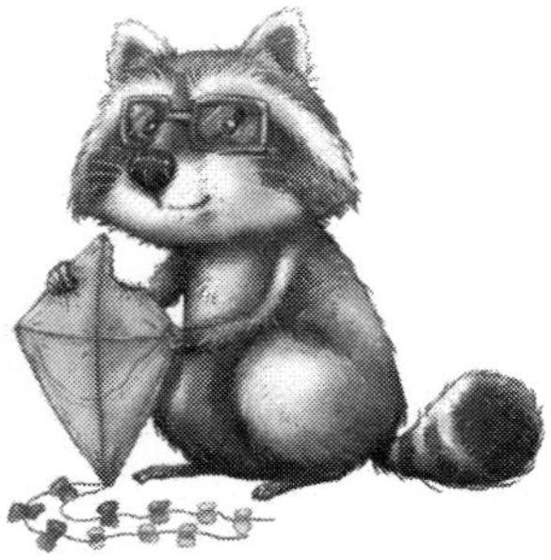

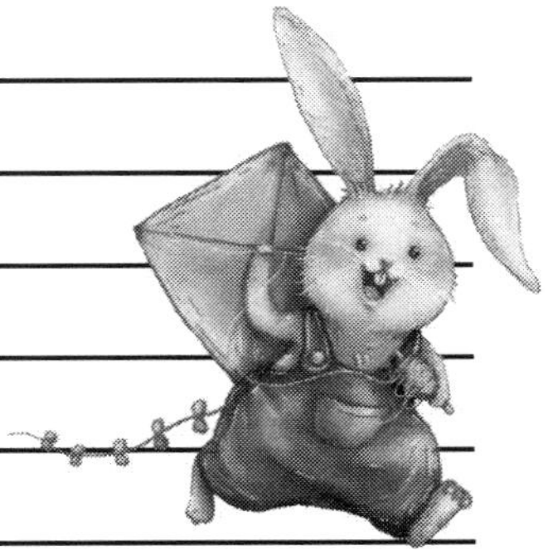

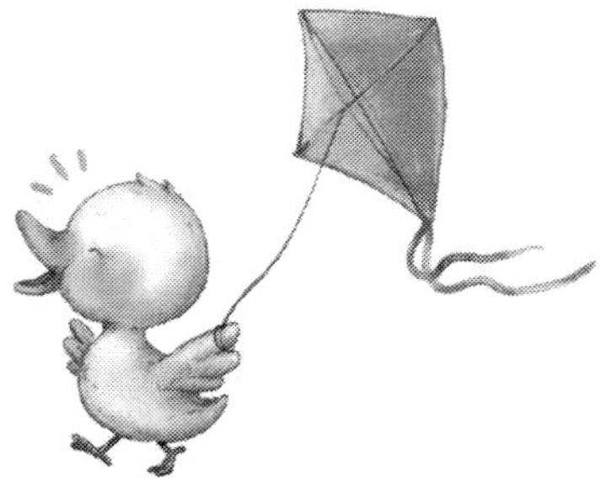

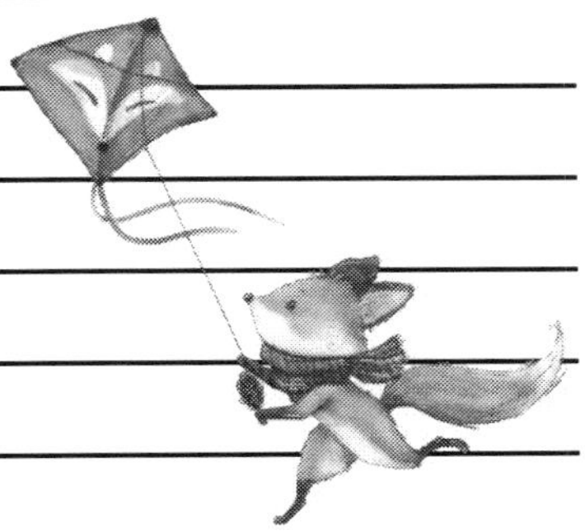

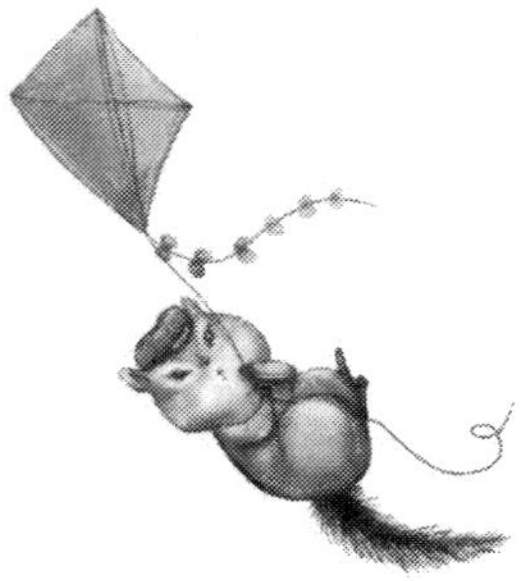

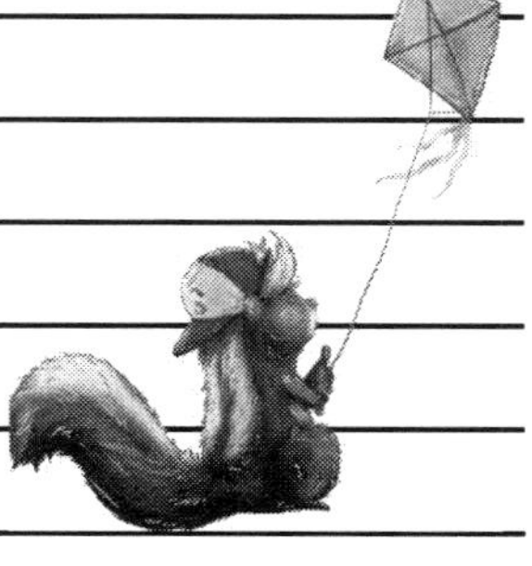

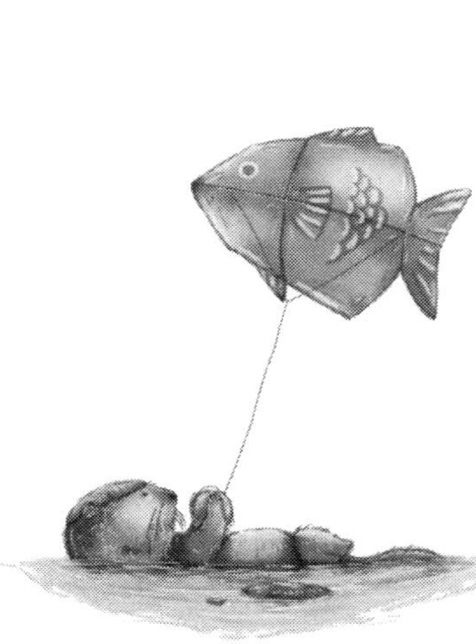

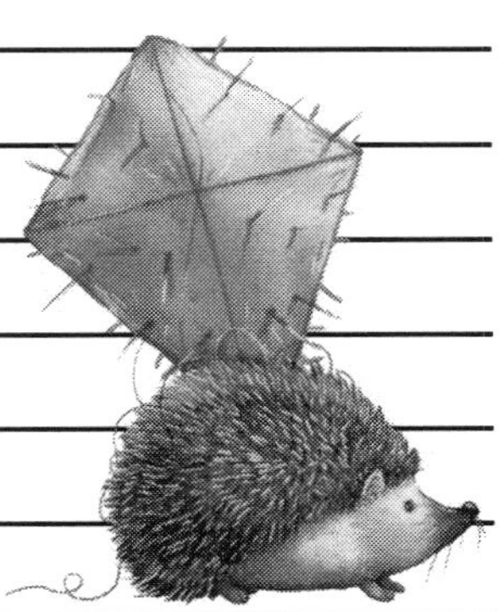

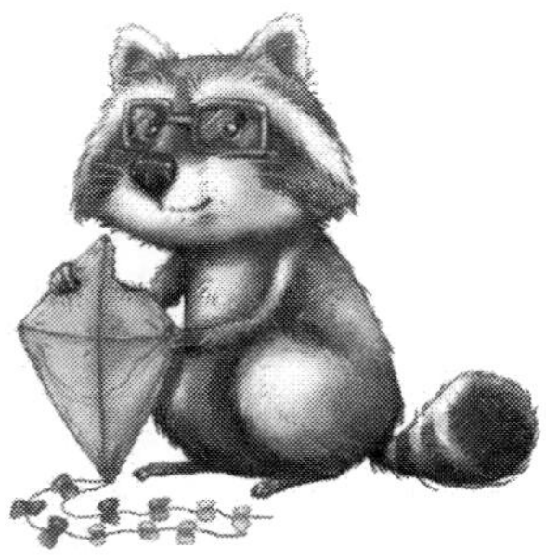

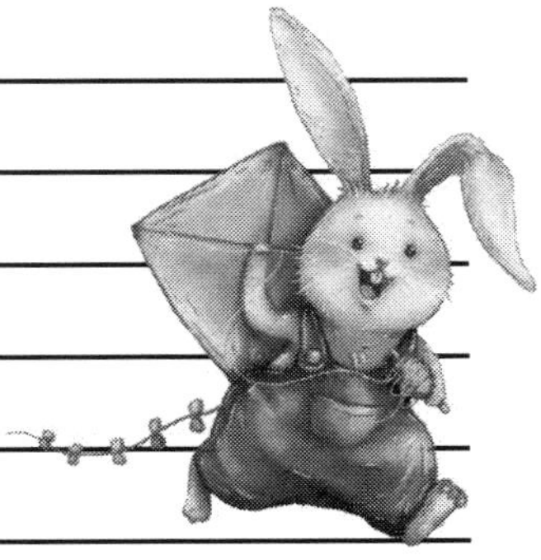

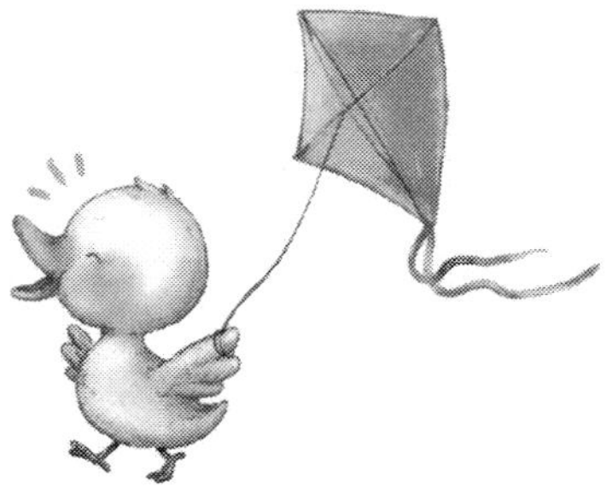

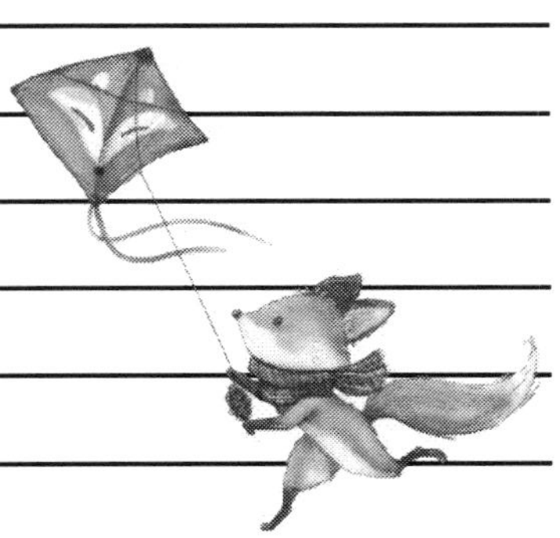

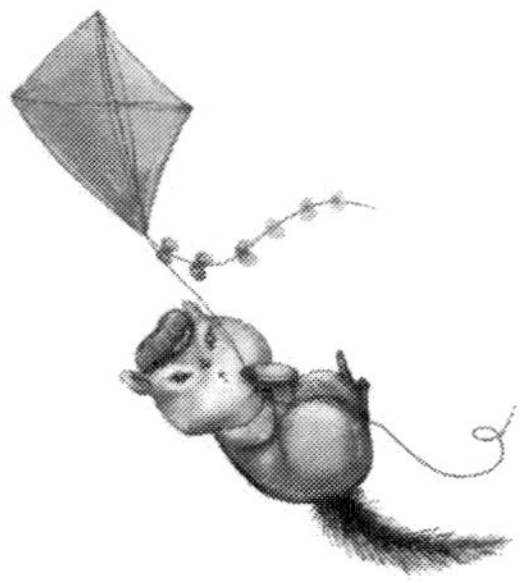

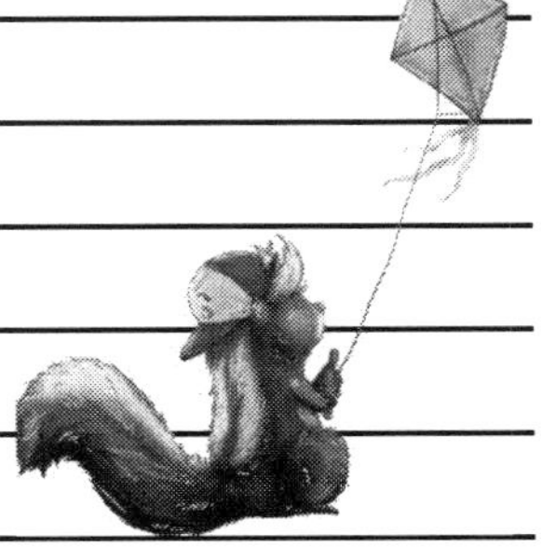

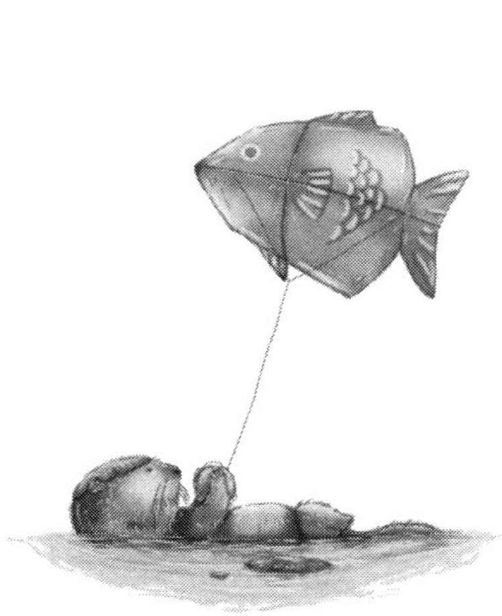

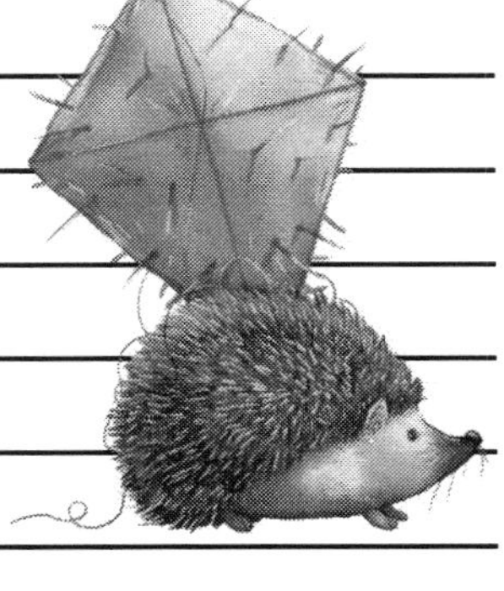

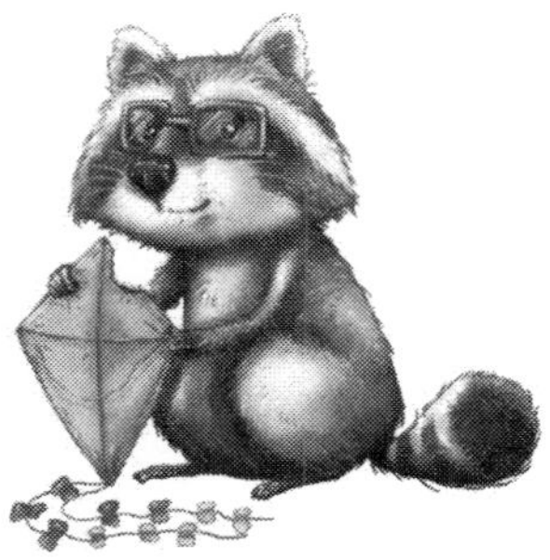

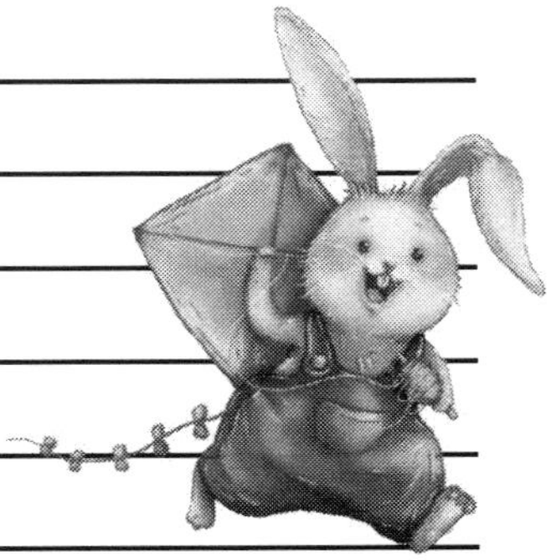

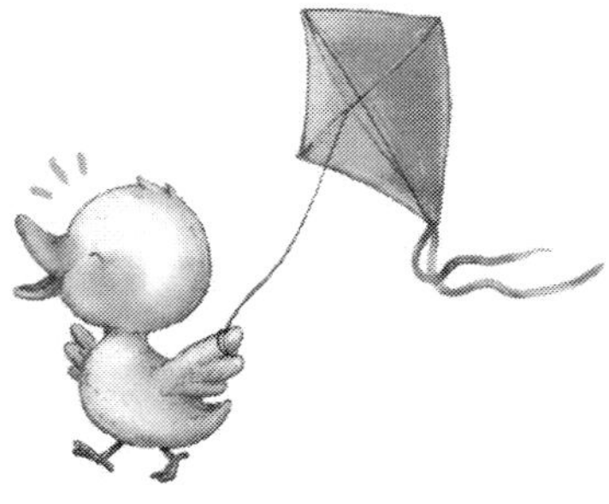

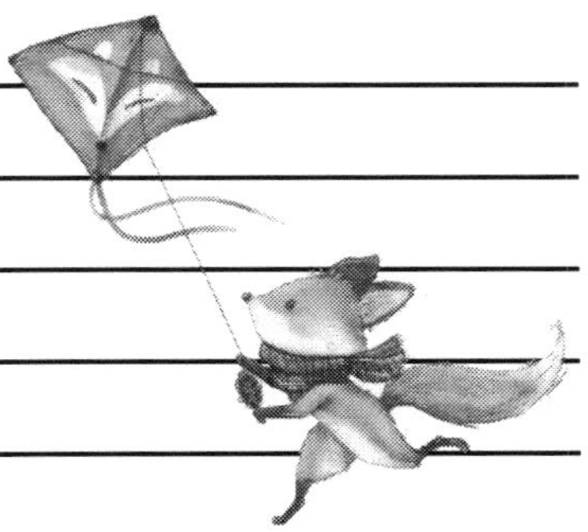

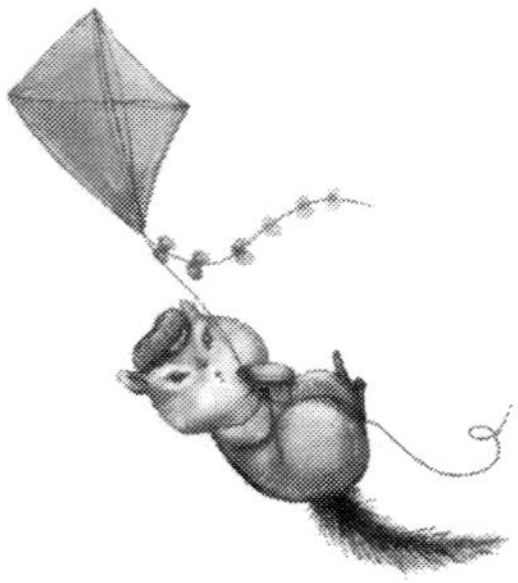

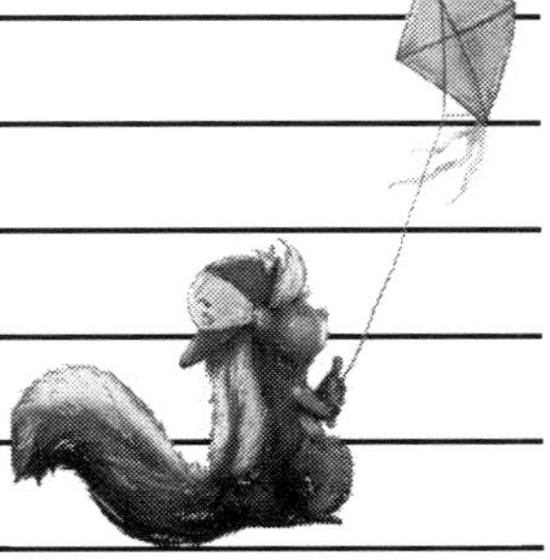

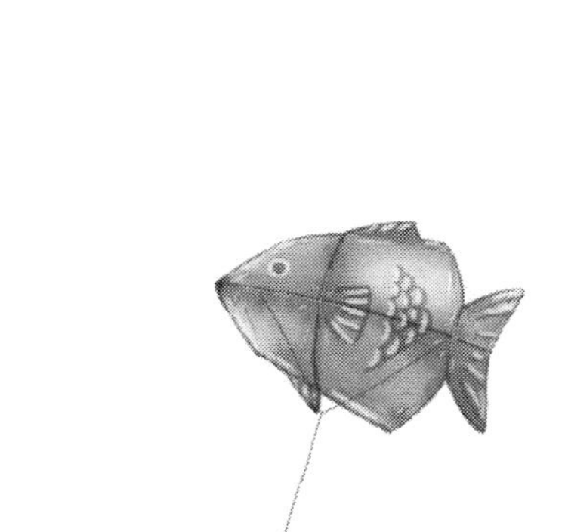

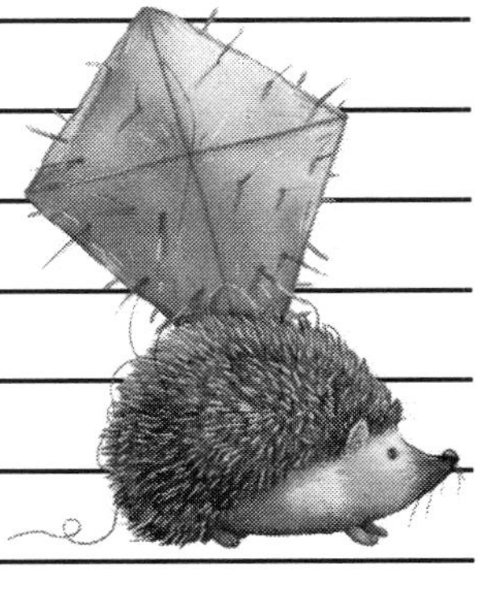

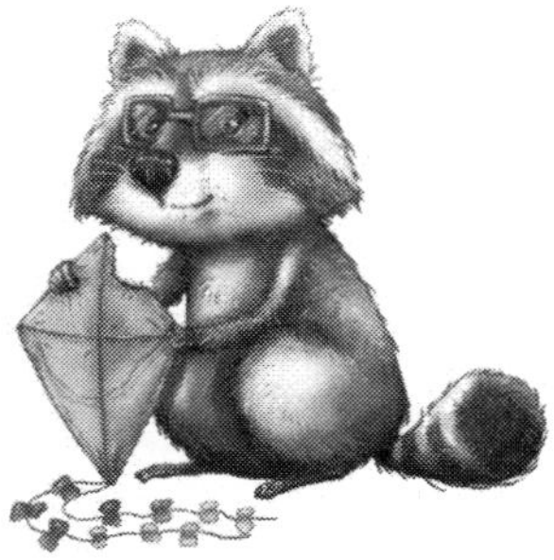

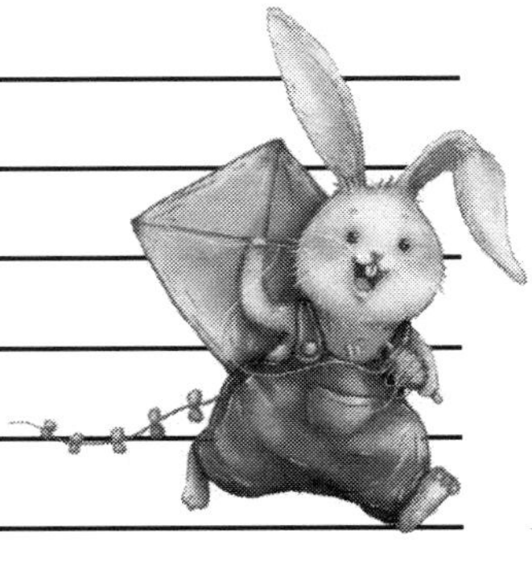

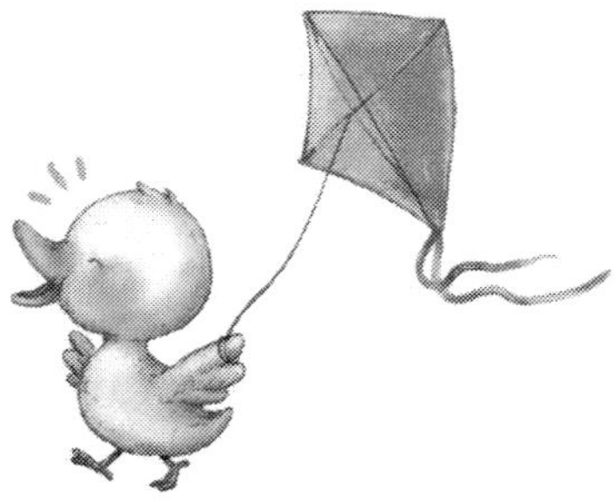

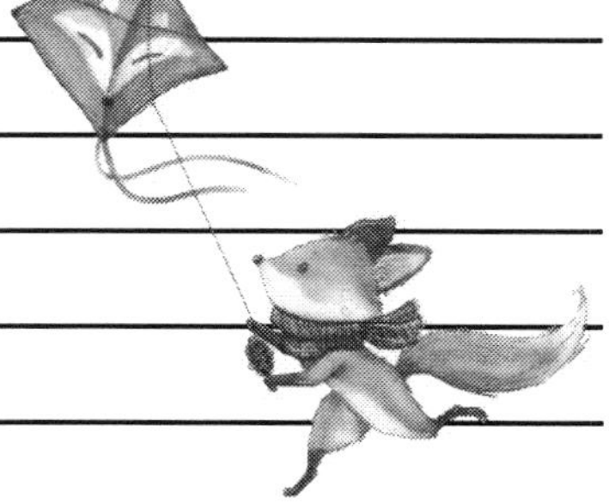

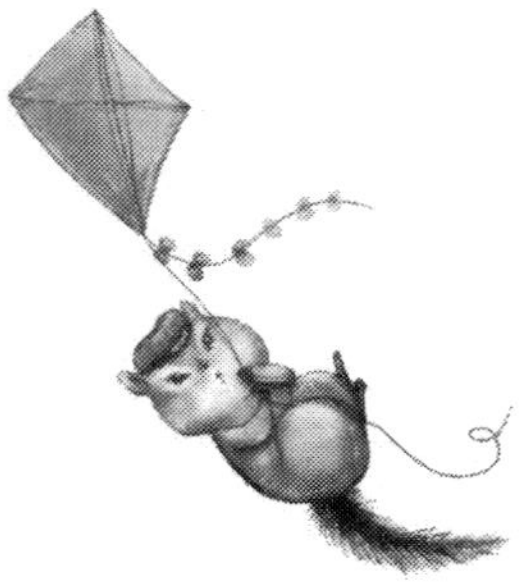

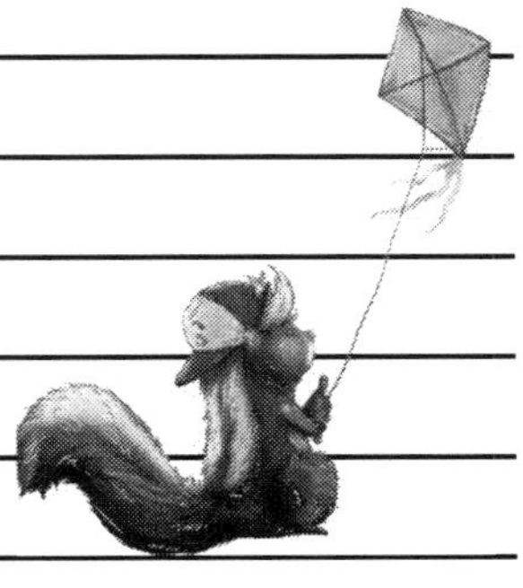

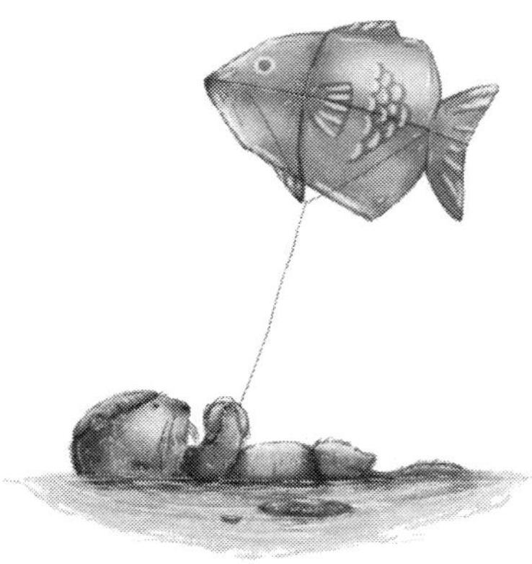

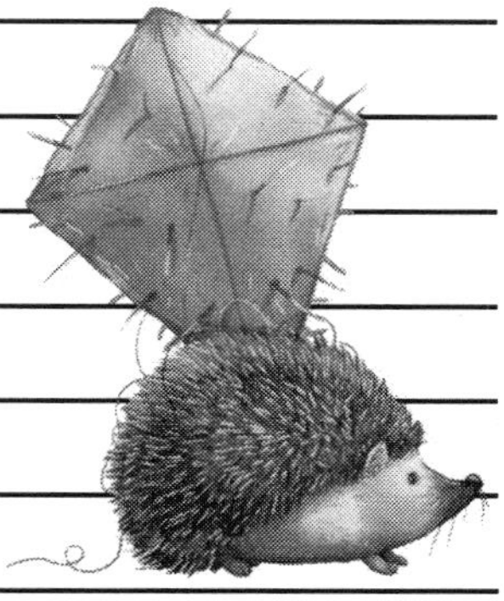

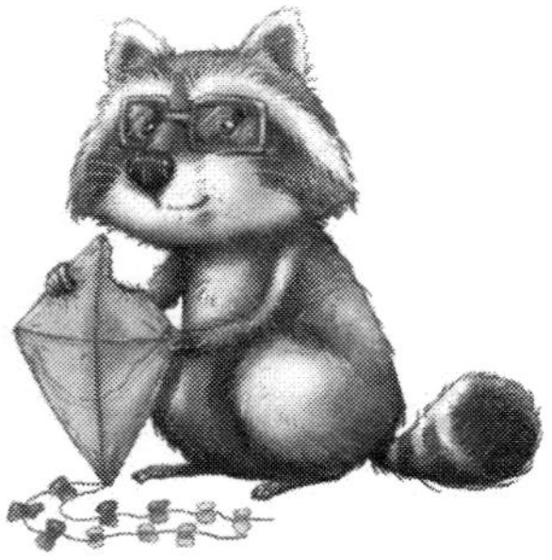

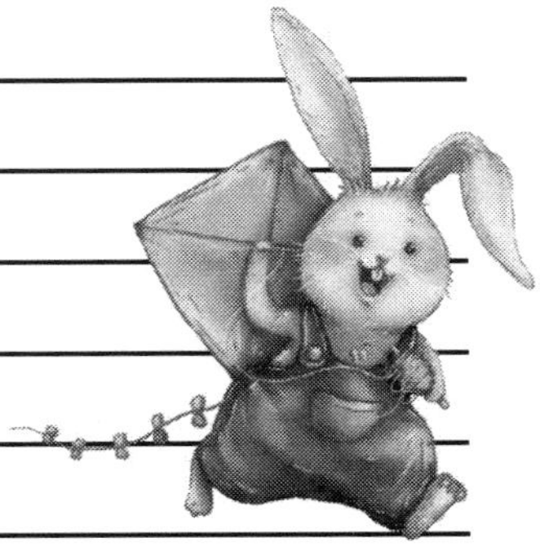

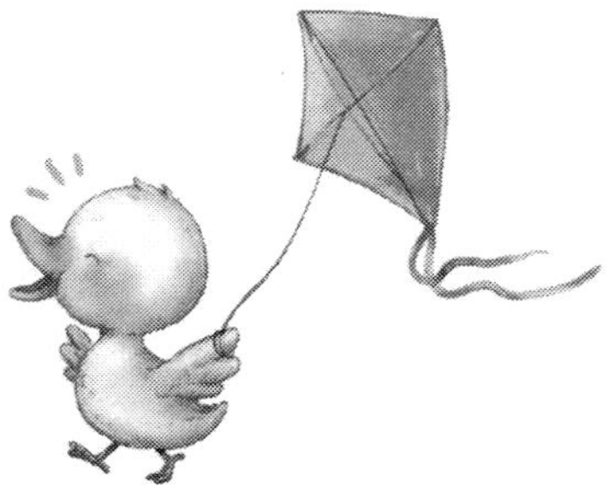

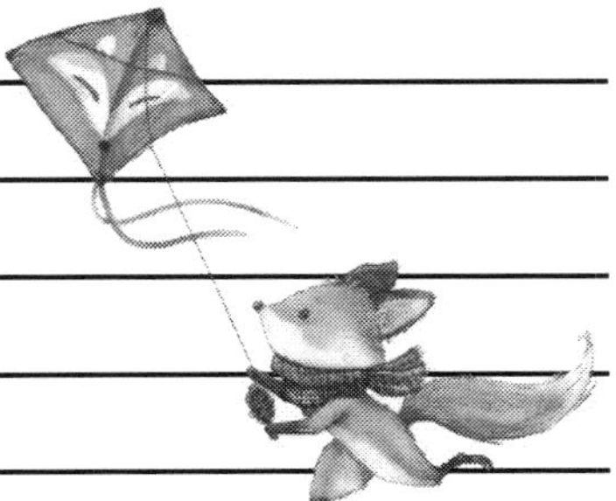

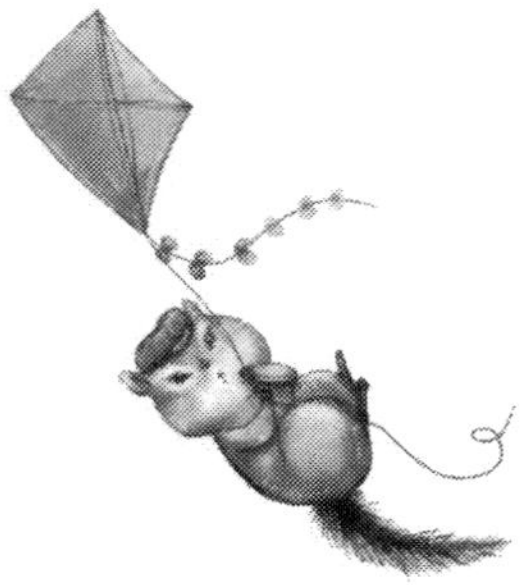

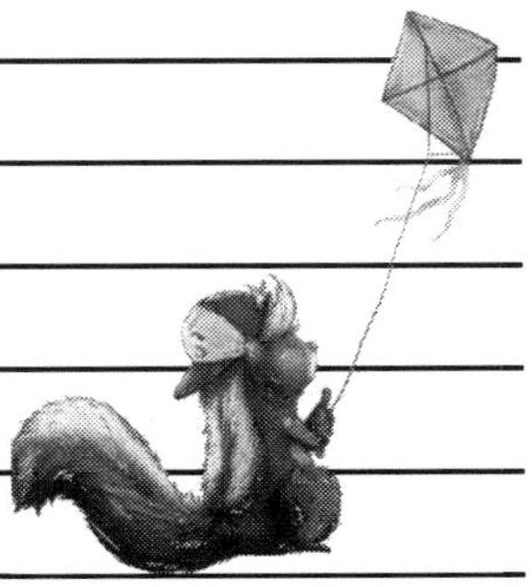

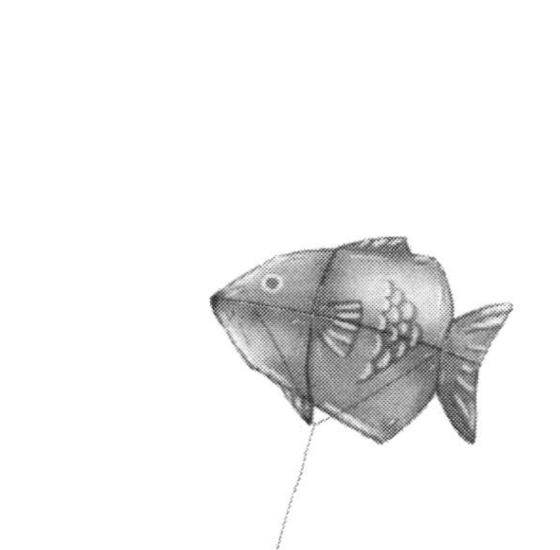

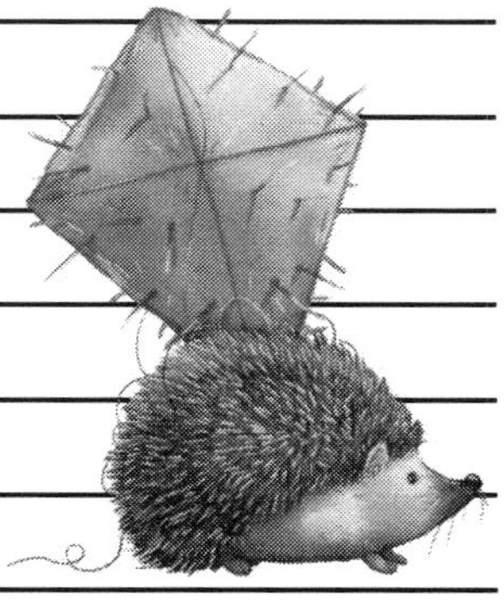

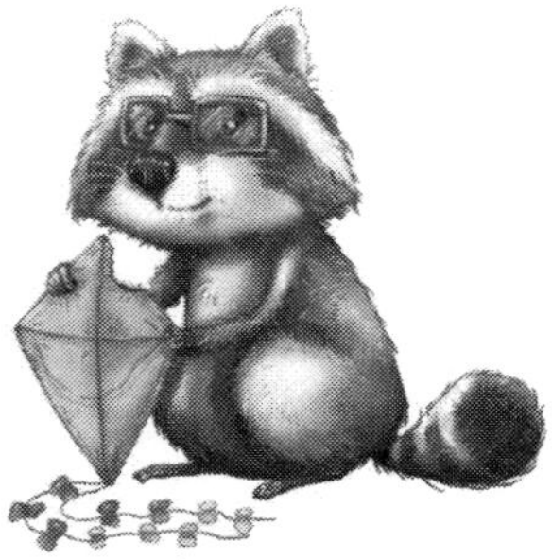

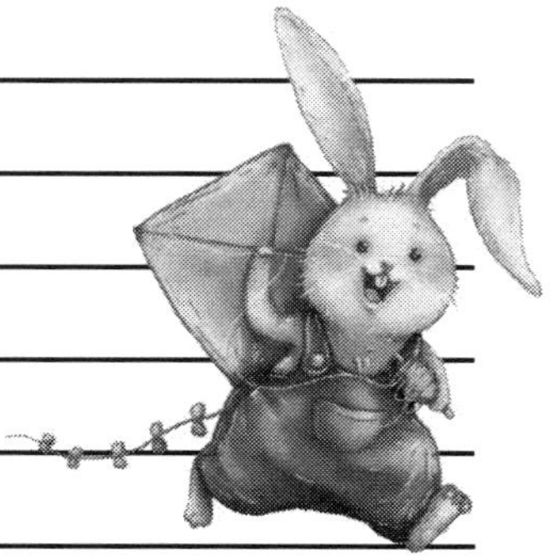

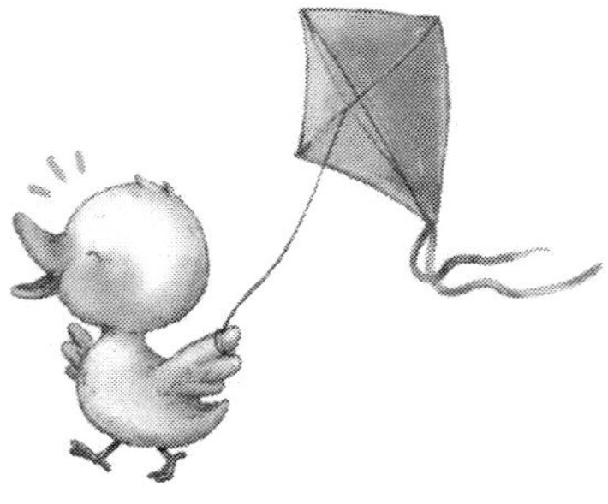

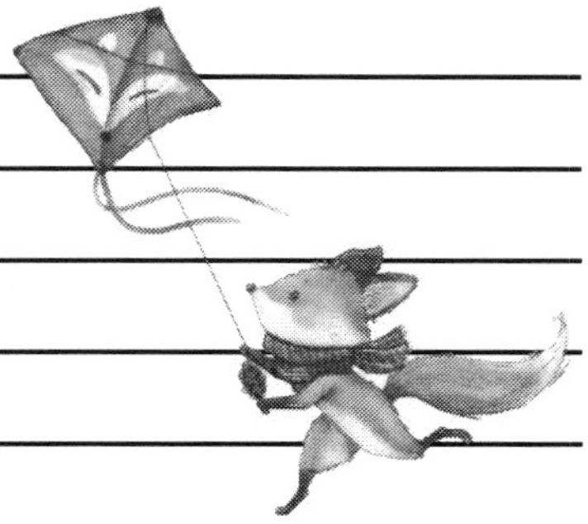

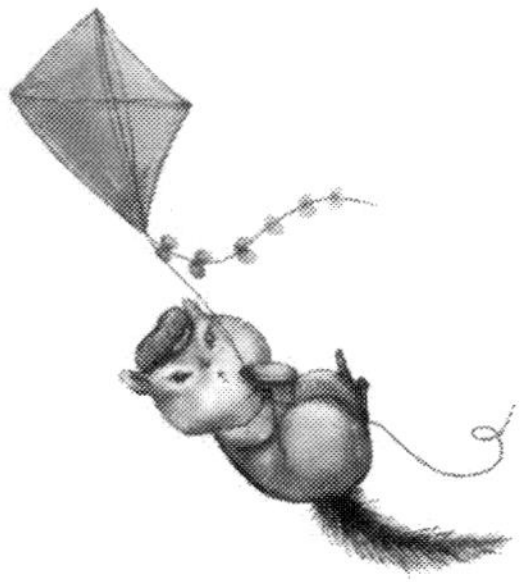

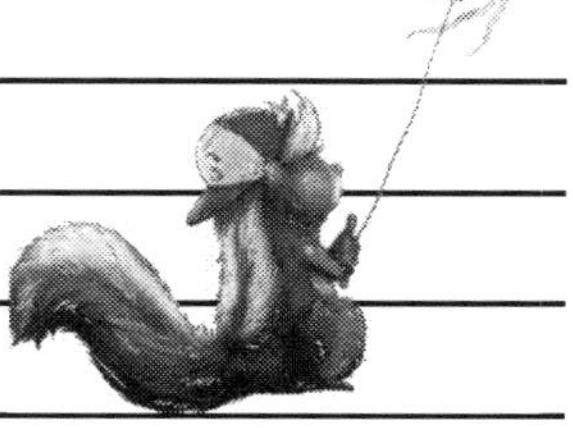

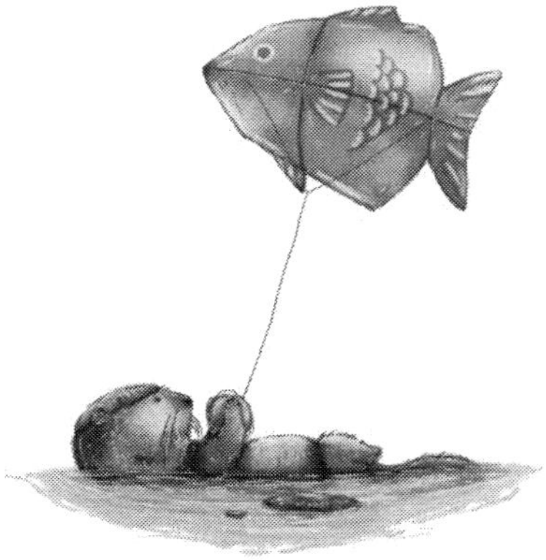

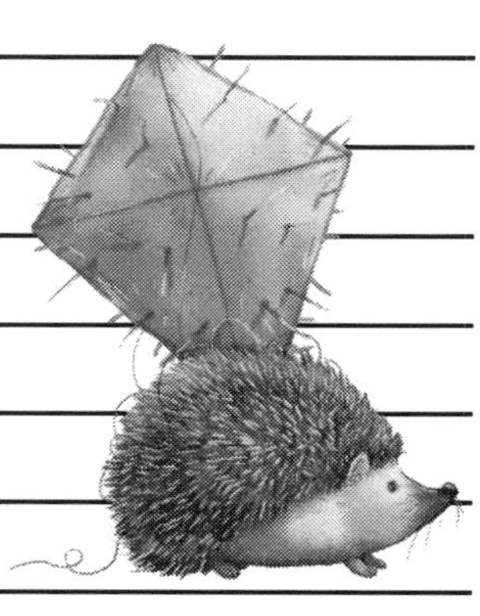

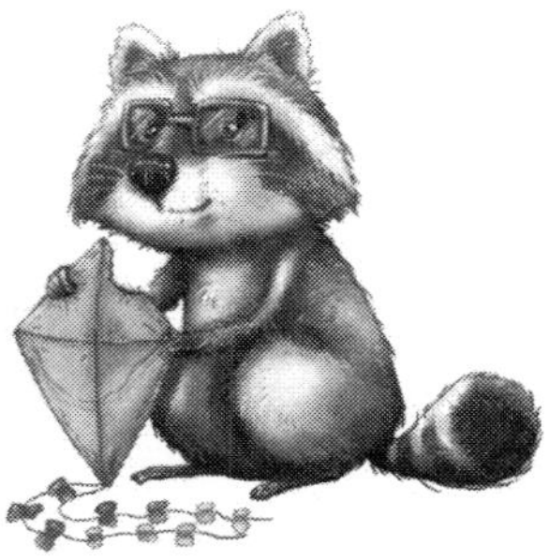

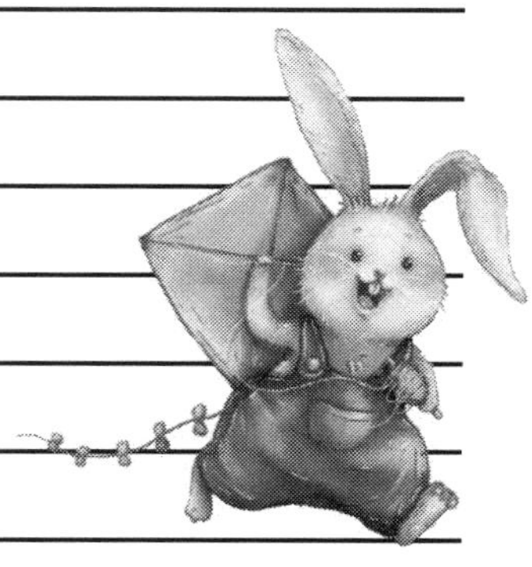

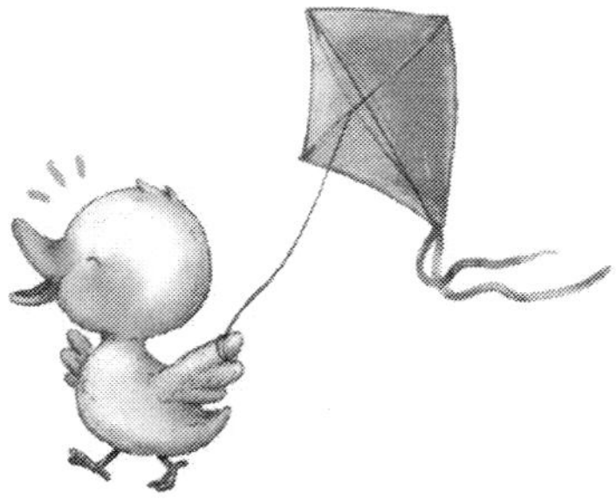

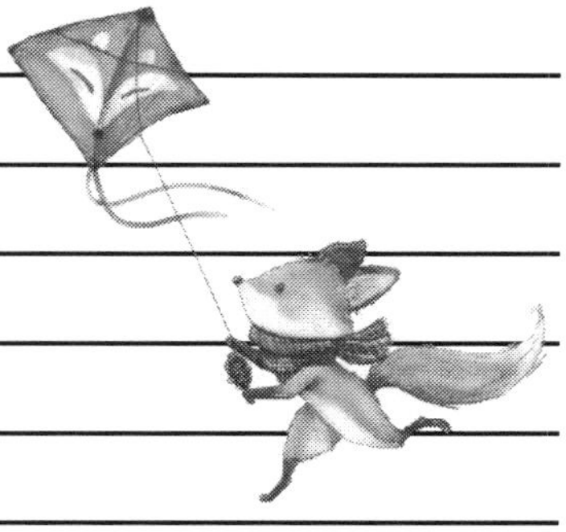

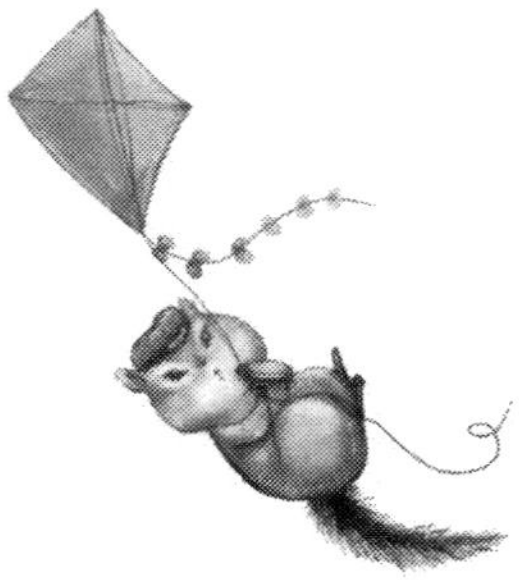

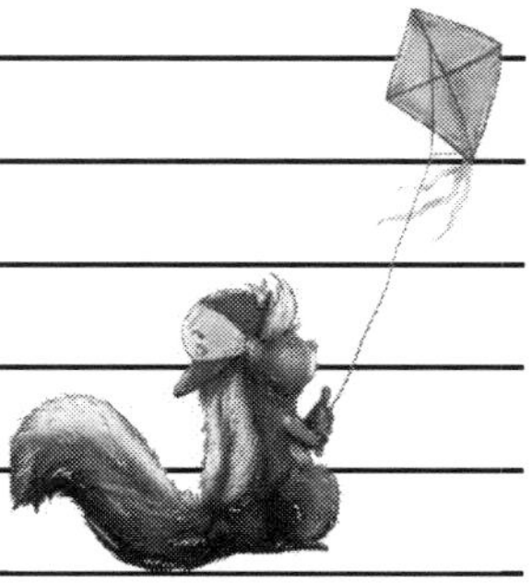

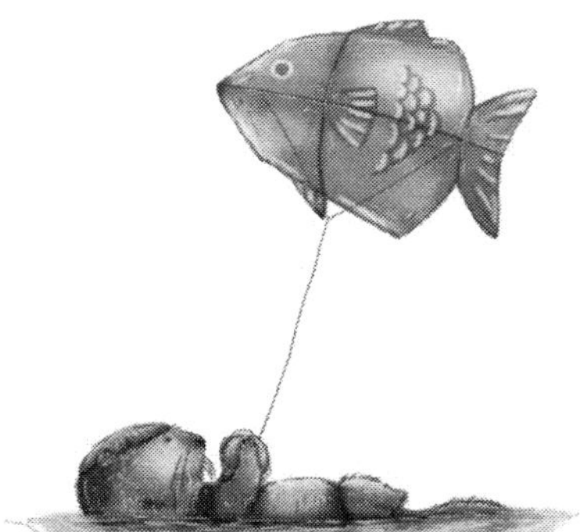

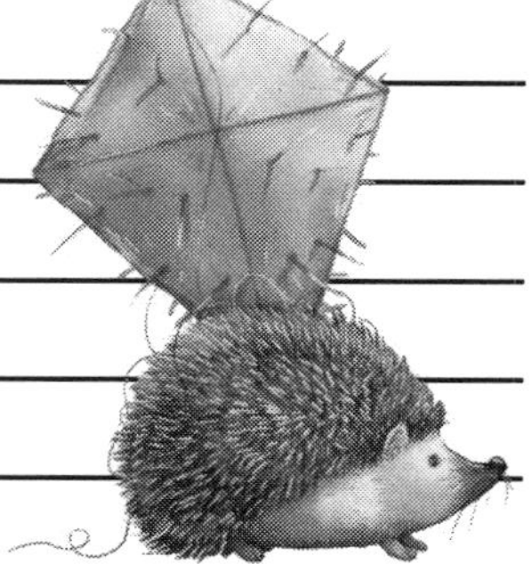

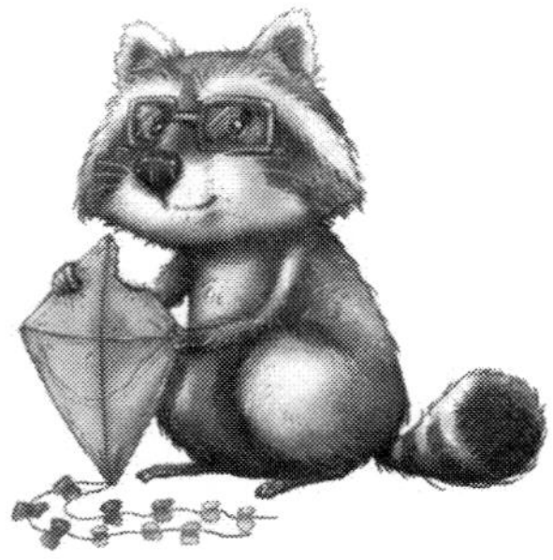

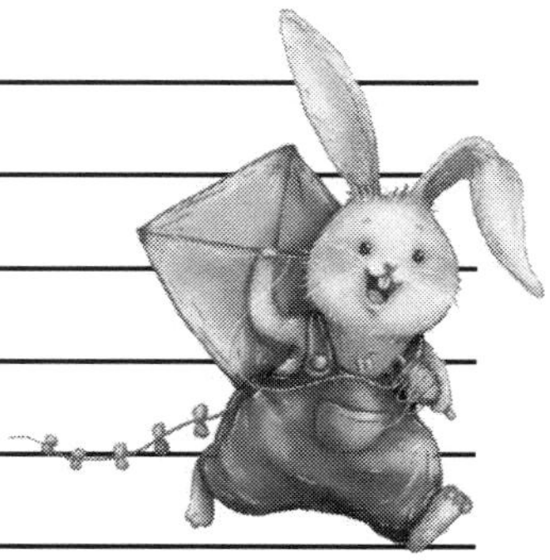

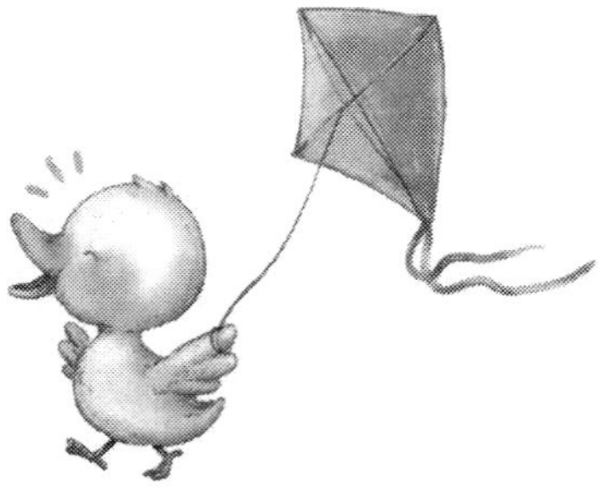

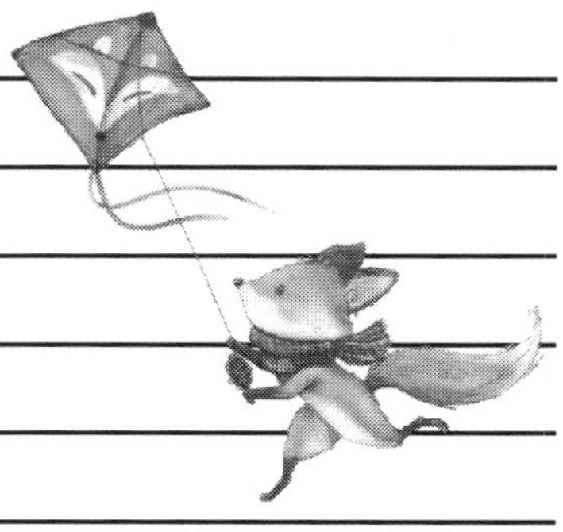

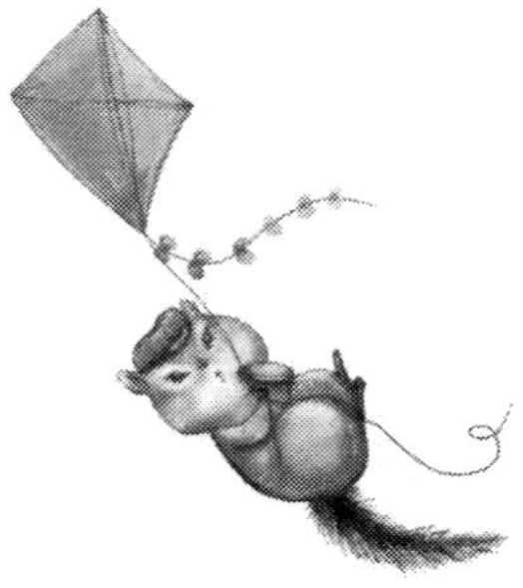

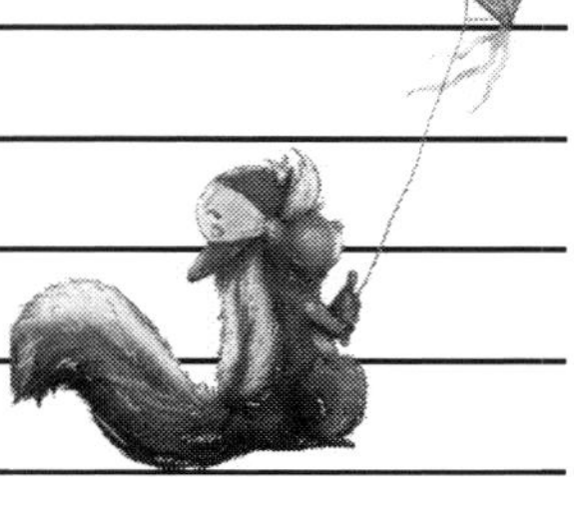

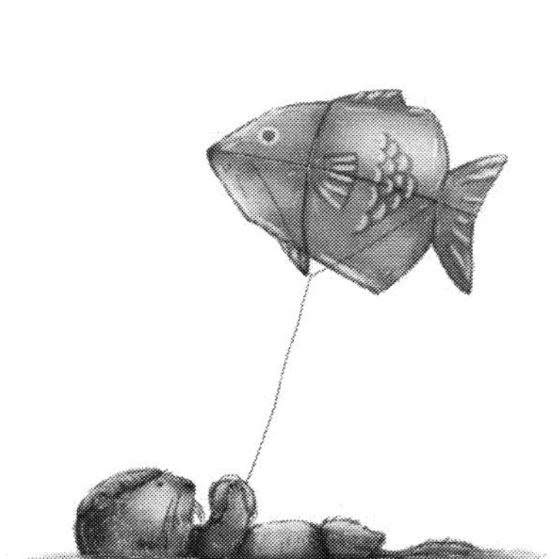

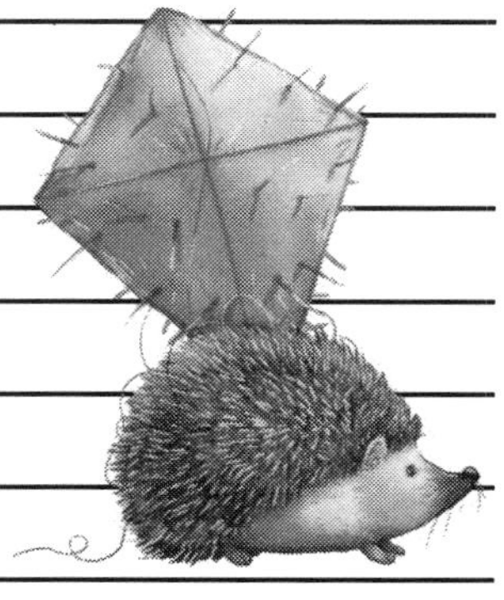

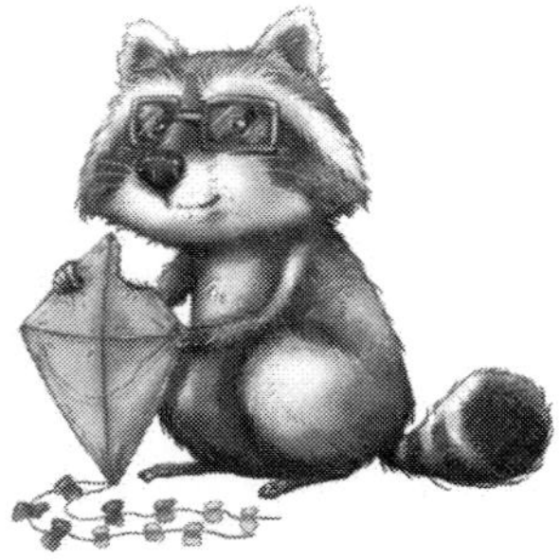

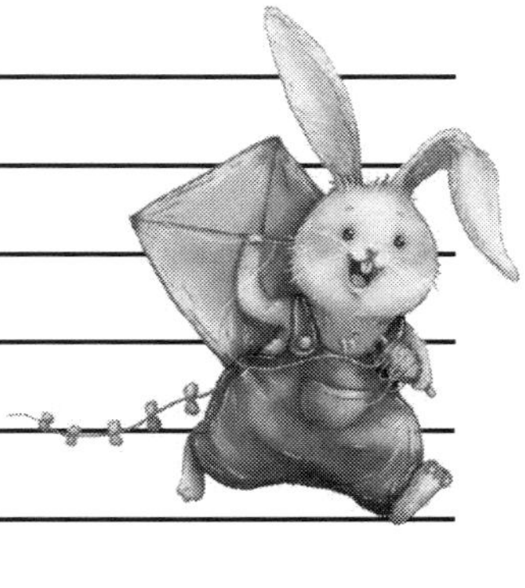

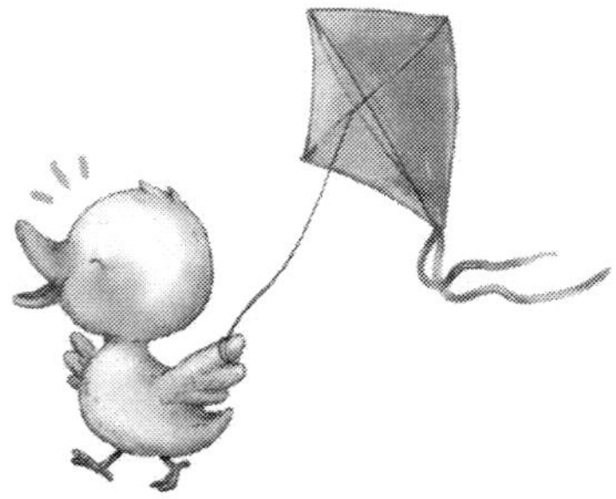

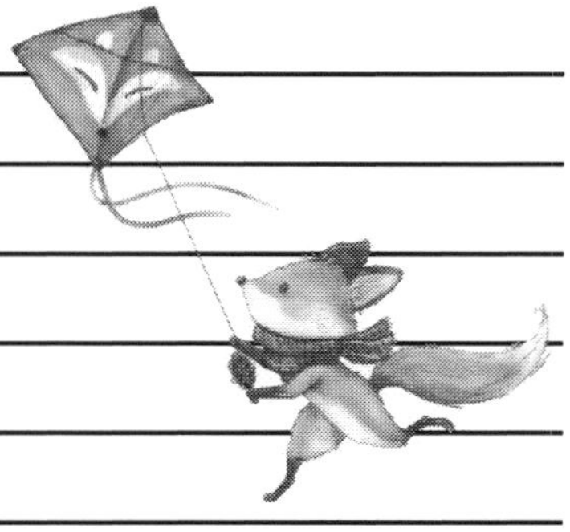

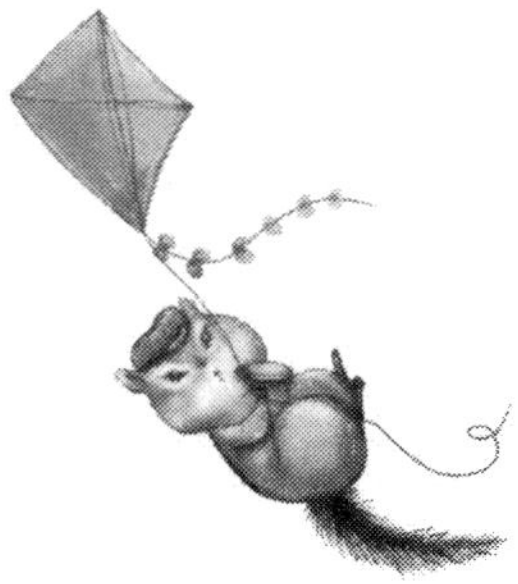

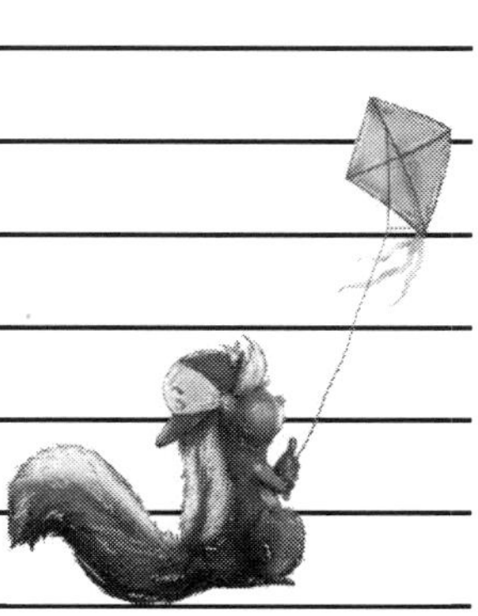

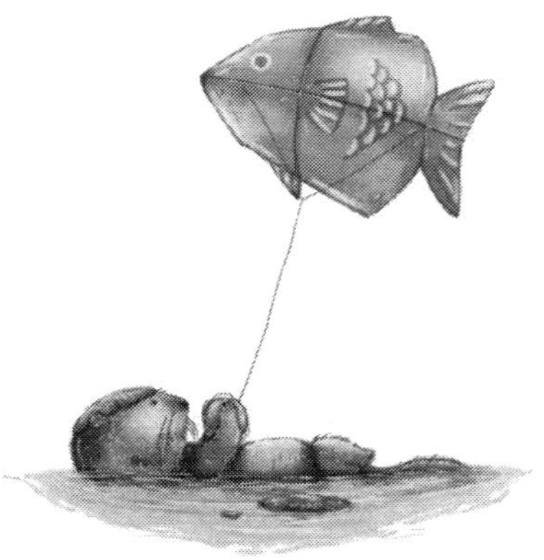

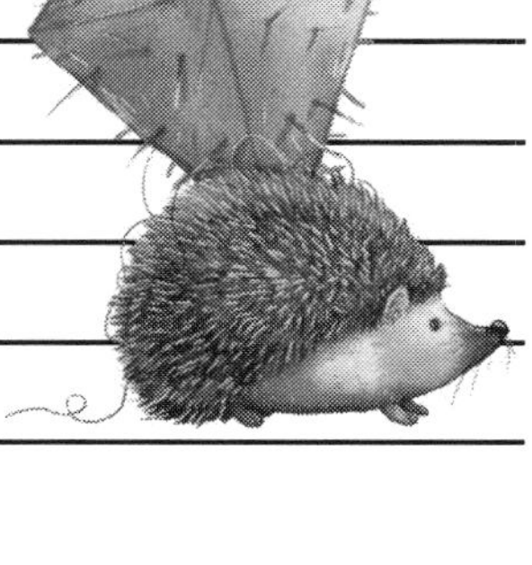

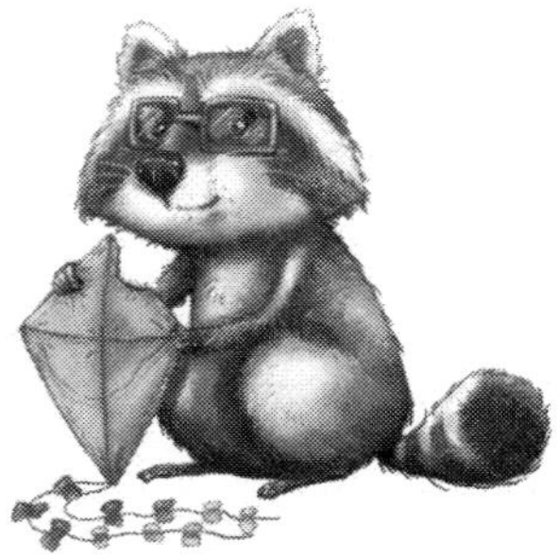

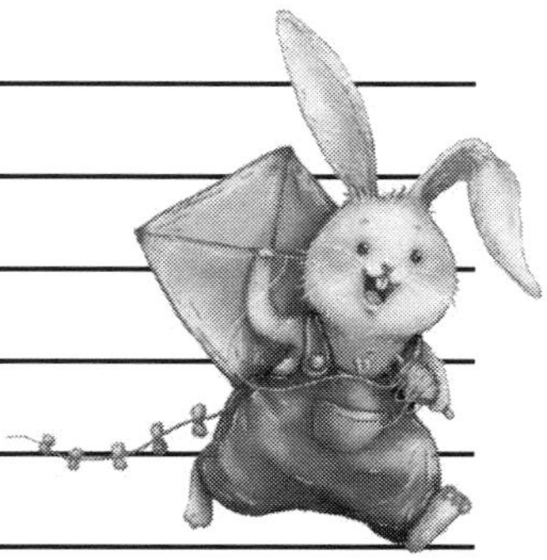

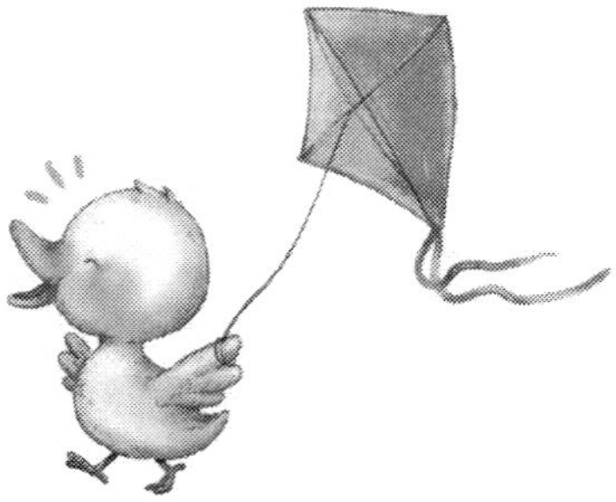

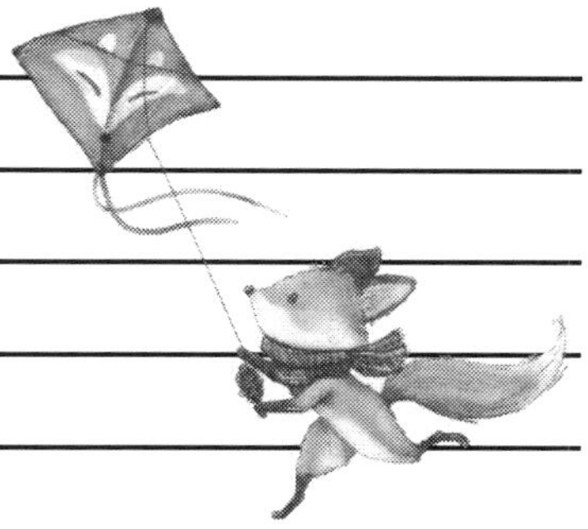

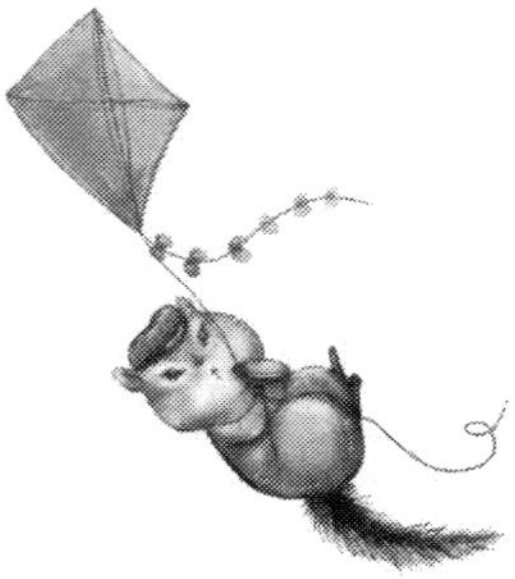

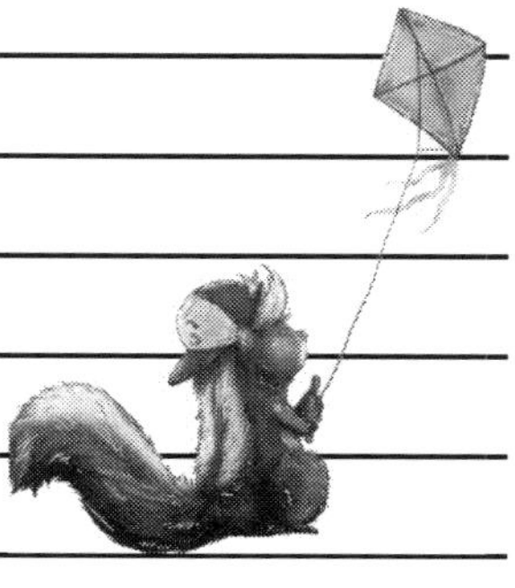

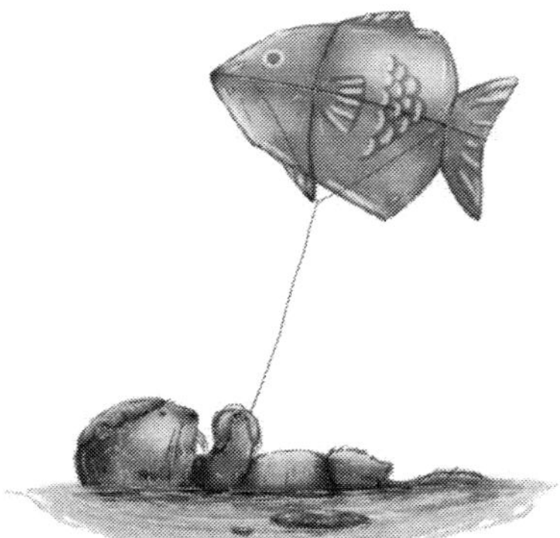

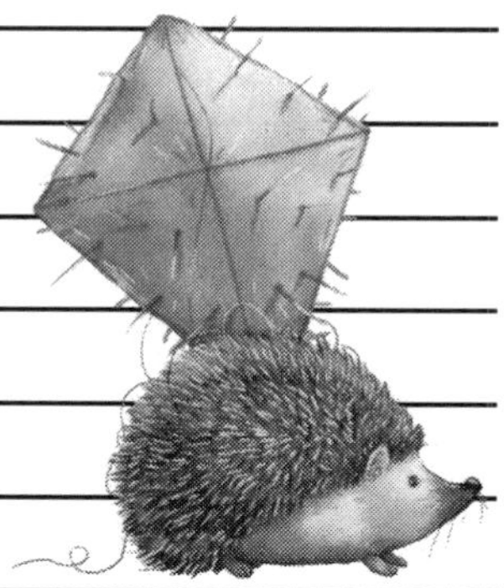

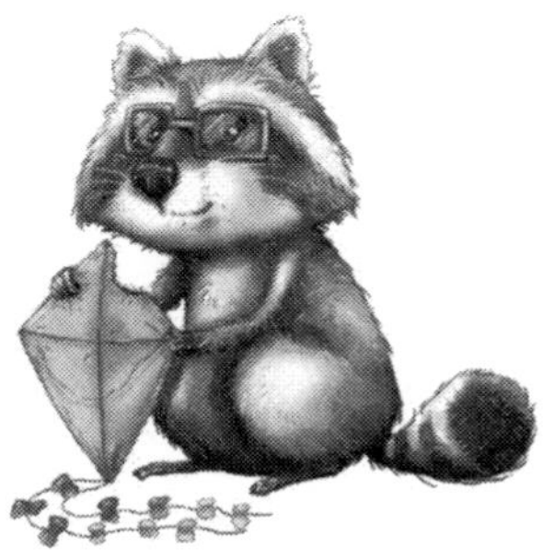

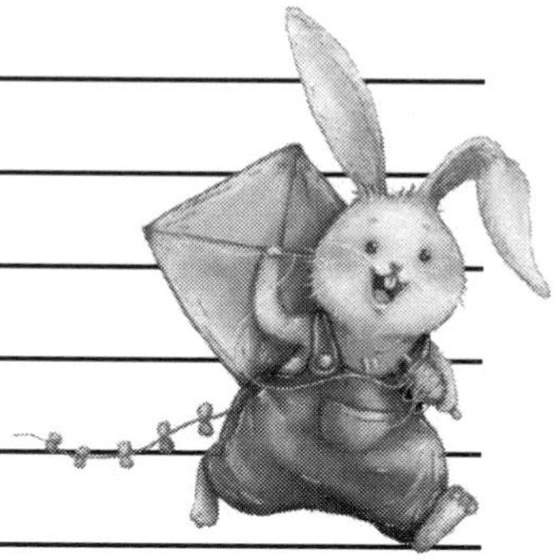

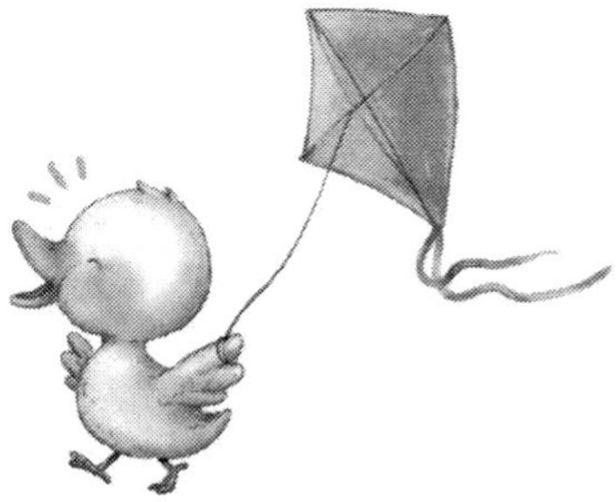

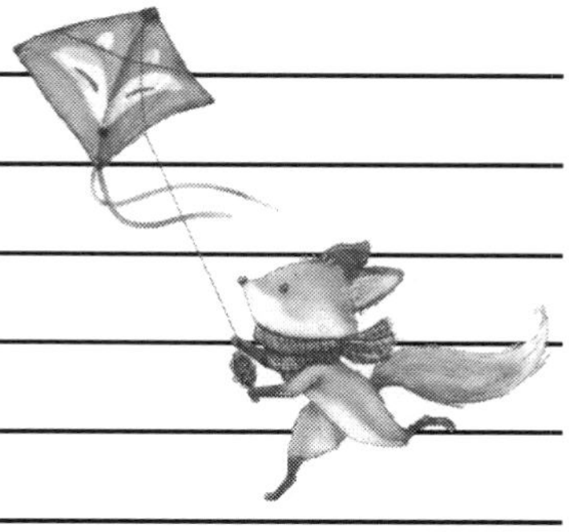

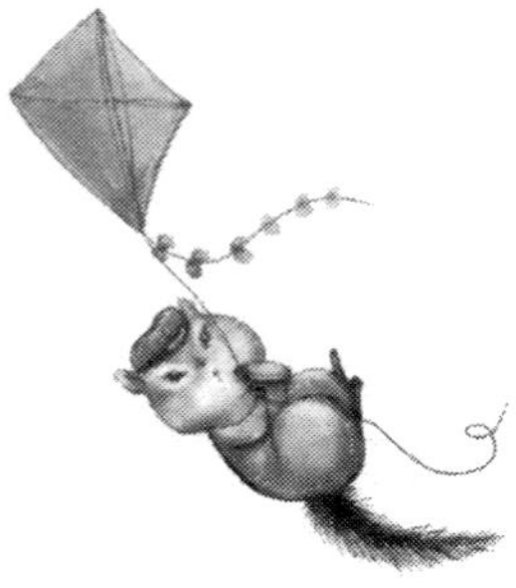

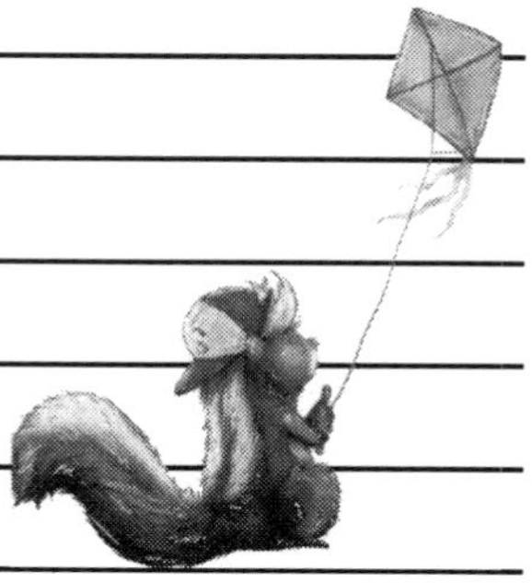

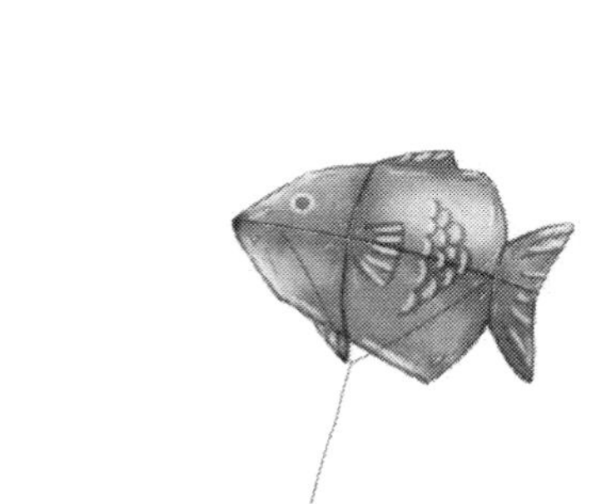

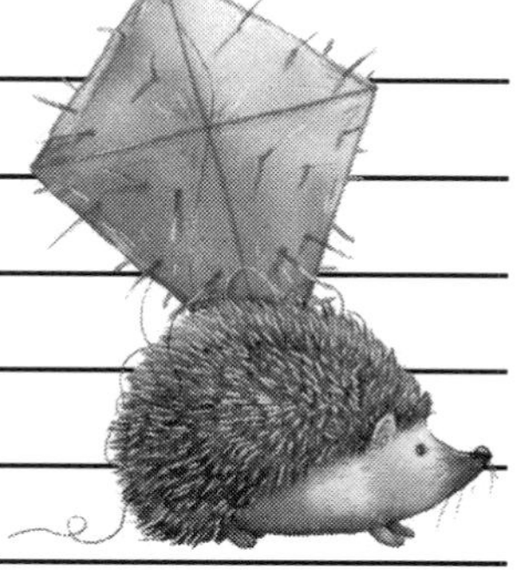

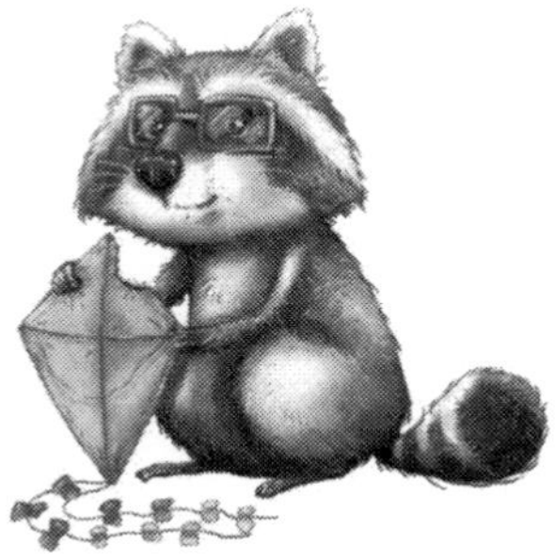

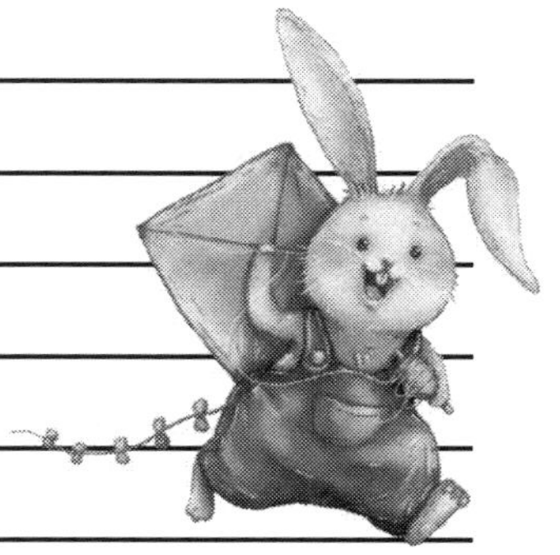

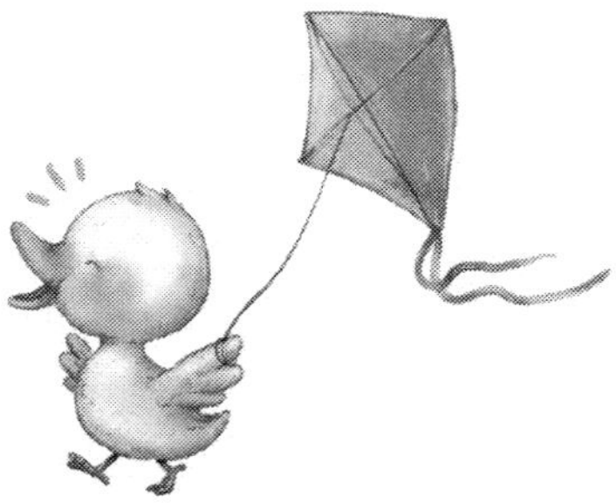

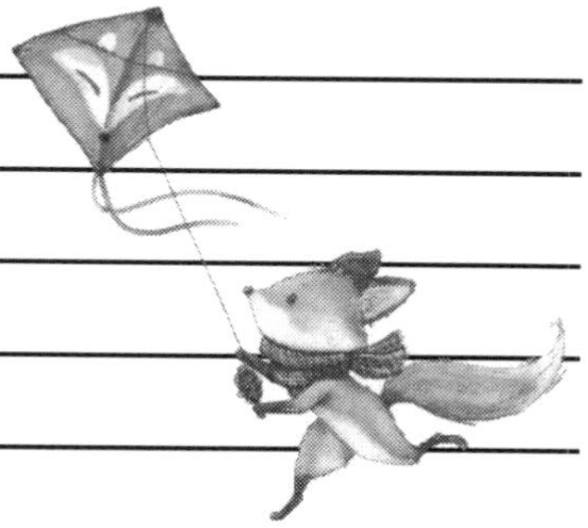

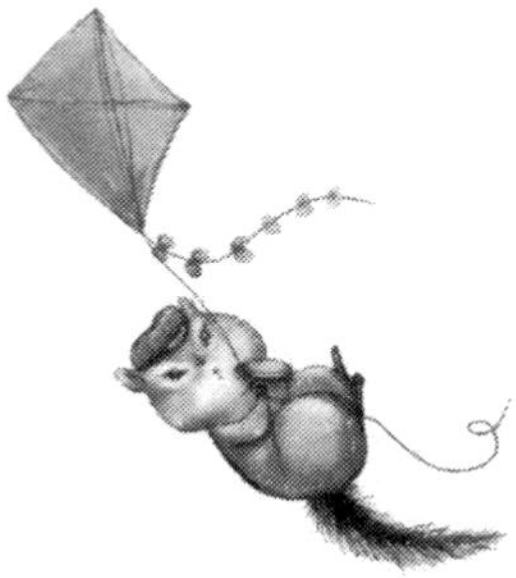

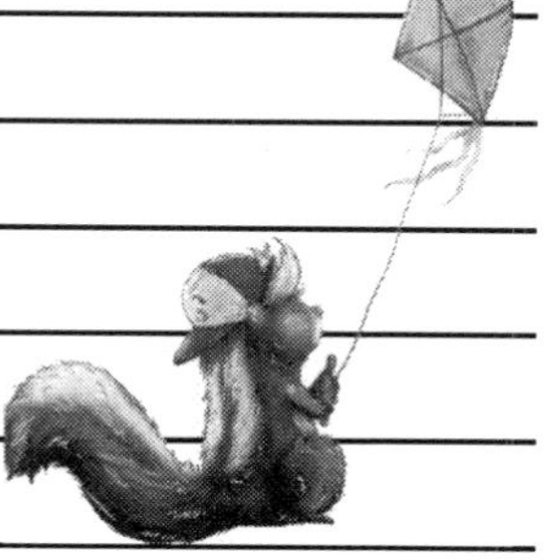

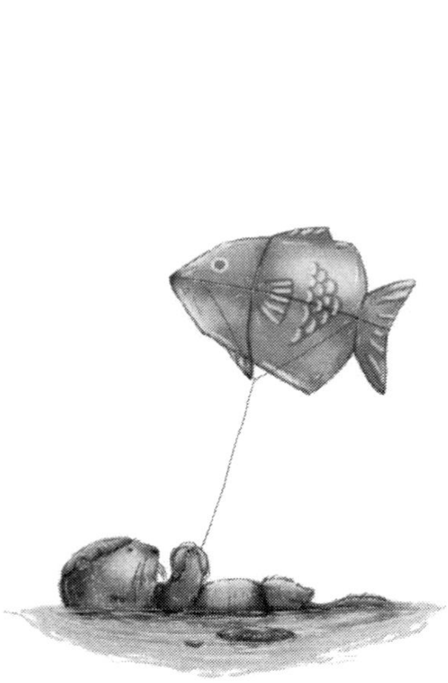

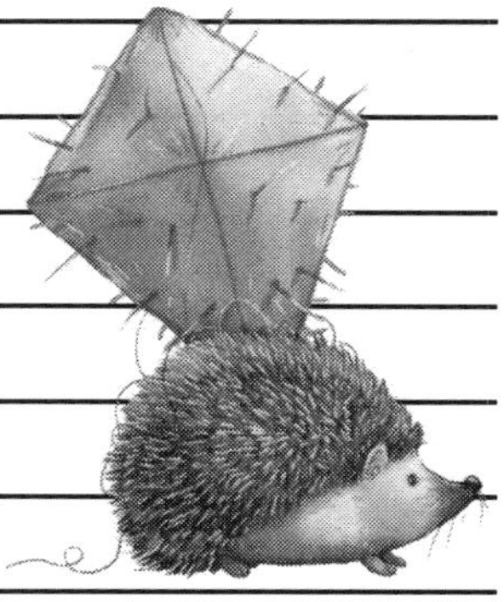

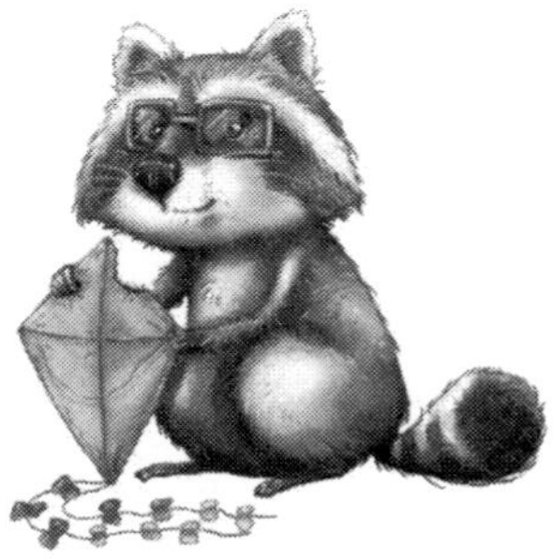

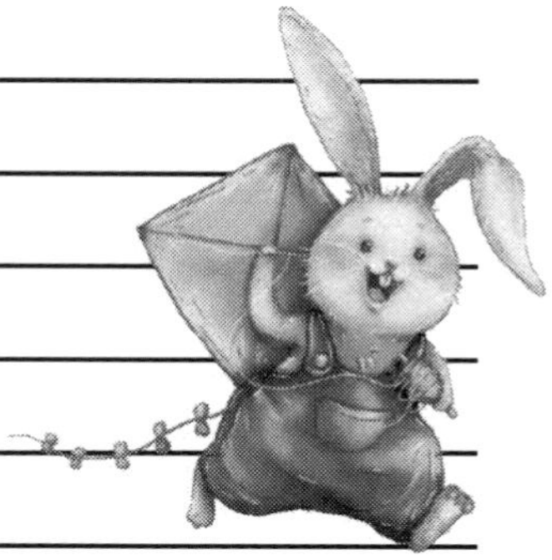

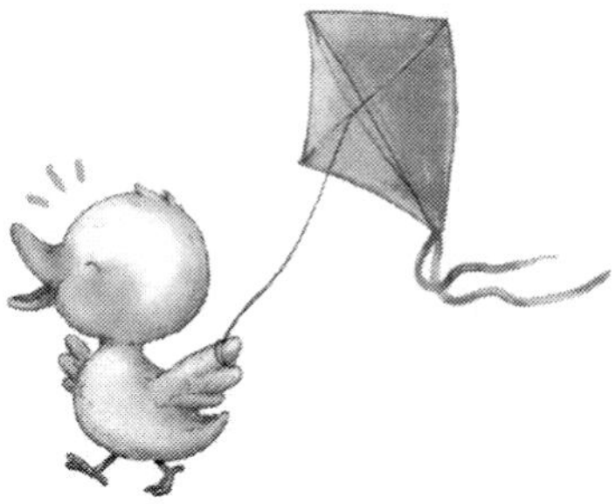

11910917R00060

Printed in Great Britain
by Amazon